Restoration of the Soul
(Pocket Size)

Restoration of the Soul (Pocket Size)

THE PRESENCE OF GOD CHANGES EVERYTHING

Bill Vincent

RWG Publishing

CONTENTS

RWG Publishing

PO Box 596

Litchfield, IL 62056

https://rwgpublishing.com/

Published in the United States of America

1

We all may have had that time in our lives where we were so tired of the fight and wanted to give up on everything. This is a fresh take on overcoming the death or darkness of our soul.

Before this thing called time ends, there's going to be geographical locations that are so saturated with the presence of the Lord that the glory of God is seen visibly by surrounding communities.

The radiance of his presence will be seen on the faces of people. There's a revelation that has started to unfold, but it's going to snowball, and that's the revelation of his goodness. There's something about the father heart of God that's about to be released to the church so that it can be released to the world.

In that revelation of his goodness, his glory will be seen. Moses asked to see the glory of the Lord, and the Lord showed him all his goodness. And he came down with his face radiant with the presence of the Lord. I believe that the Lord is changing the face of his church through a revelation of his goodness. He's going to change how we see, how we think. He's changing how we appear even to the people around us, to the communities, our role in community life, in city life, in national life. And it's coming out of an understanding and experience with his goodness. It's a deep and profound thing that he's doing, and it's good.

He said in Psalms 67 there's this prayer for the light of God's face to shine upon us, that his way would be known in the earth, that the face of the Lord, the favor of God would be seen upon people so that his ways, what he is like, would be revealed all over the earth. The Lord wants to reveal his goodness to you to change your countenance so that your countenance will testify to them that he is good. There's something about the blessing of the Lord, resting upon people, that is just simply increasing and increasing.

It's really a big deal that we realize that the farther you go with God, the less you can take with you. And there's an exchange that takes place as you yield, as we yield ourselves, yield our agendas, our purposes, even our well-built agendas that are modeled after what we think should happen in the world, even those things as we lay them down before the Lord, and he begins to share that countenance of his pleasure, that countenance of his goodness, that countenance of his glory, the radiance of his glory over you, over me. It changes. It changes how we think. It changes how we live, how we act. It changes what we do with our life.

I feel like the Lord is releasing a measure of glory to make ministry easier. I don't know if that's the right way to put it, "to make ministry easier." Let me say it this way. He's releasing his glory integrated with the weightiness of his presence. He's called the father of glory, so all glory is his. All glory emanates from his person. As the father of glory's releasing the weightiness of his presence... The weightiness, that which the heaviness, the heavy goodness. Sometimes we think of heaviness as a heavy burden. The weighty goodness of God resting on people, because he's wanted to reveal himself. He's not happy with the lies that people believe. He's not happy with the misrepresentation. Do you know what it means to take his name in vain? It's much bigger than cursing, using a curse word. It's to misrepresent him. It's to stand in his name and not to represent accurately.

I think the whole thing of there being a glorious church, the people of God caring, that manifest presence of the Lord, that radiance of his glory, is the strongest evangelistic tool there is. The Lord wants you to be blessed. He wants you to be blessed. That doesn't mean owning mansions on a hilltop and all the other stuff. It means that every part of your life is just touched with the blessing and the favor of God. Everything gets immersed in favor, and it's legal to have favor here. You don't have to apologize for it. You don't have to explain it away. You don't have to feel guilty for it. You don't have to explain it to somebody who wonders.

When you have it, it's yours to give. It's when you have favor, it's yours to give. It's a strange thing, but we actually get positioned by the Lord before humanity to begin to release favor. It's not as though we earned it. It's not as though we did anything to get it. It's not as though we fasted long enough, prayed hard enough, read the Bible enough to ever deserve it. It just all comes from his goodness. I just think it's an increasing manifestation of his grace that he's going to reveal in the earth.

All of this has to do with the presence of the Lord, the manifest presence of King Jesus resting upon, abiding upon his people. It's the most wonderful thing to be the worshiper and to have the Lord liberally release glory to rest upon a people. There's a weightiness in the room that wasn't here at the beginning, the weightiness of presence. And the fascinating thing to me is that, as we learn to live and abide and function in this presence that is only set to increase if we steward well, things just happen. It's unexplainable, but it just happens.

I've shaken somebody's hand, just put my hand on their shoulder, and blessed them. Not doing anything, no great, noble act, no stirring of great faith, no prophetic degree. Just being nice and to have the curse of migraines broken off of them just not even knowing there was a problem, but it's the byproduct of hosting the presence. It has nothing at all to do with great faith. That has a role, but there are just times when the weightiness of presence becomes so strong that the shadow does heal. We've had it happen just walking by a person, where all that afflicts them just is gone.

I want to stir the appetite for the presence, to recognize, you know, he's always here in that sense. He said he'd never leave us or forsake us. If you take the presence of the Lord in the graduated ways he has revealed, we know first of all that the presence of God holds everything together. Every cell, every molecule is held in place by the presence of the Lord. It says, in Colossians, "He holds all things together." So, in that sense, he is everywhere. He isn't the tree, but he holds the tree together. The pantheists worship the tree, thinking it is God because everything is God. That's not true. They are close, but no cigar. He's in the tree. He holds it all together. So, he's everywhere in that sense.

But then, something happens when you become born again. God was already in me in the sense that he held every cell of my person together, but when I received Christ, the spirit of God actually took up residence in me in an unrealized way. Or, not unrealized. Unexperienced, not experienced, wasn't a reality before receiving Christ, before surrendering to Christ.

I don't know what this means, but I've seen this in the scripture of late. It's in the Gospel of John, and I don't know. I'm going to write about this at some point in the hopefully near future. But Jesus actually made this statement after he announced that the Holy Spirit would be taking up residence in us. He announced that he, both he and the father, would come and dwell with us. That's mind-boggling. "The Holy Spirit dwells in me." I mean, that one's already mind-boggling enough, and then he makes the declaration that the father and the son would also make their abode with us. Fascinating. Incomprehensible.

So, this presence of the Lord takes up residence in us as we surrender to Christ. Then he goes on, and he said, "Where two or more are gathered, there I am in the midst." Even though he was already with me before we ever came together, as soon as we come together in agreement in his name, there's an increased manifestation of his presence.

I want to encourage you... You can learn to recognize the increased measures of presence, of glory. Why go through life without recognizing? Why go through life without recognizing the single greatest treasure we've been given? That's himself. Why go through the Christian routine, hoping to please somebody that's out there when, in fact, you can see, recognize, feel, touch, taste of the manifest presence of the king of glory who is with you in increasing measure? When two or three gather in his name, there he is — the increased manifestation of his presence.

Then it goes on, and it says, "When we give him praise when we declare his greatness when we lift up that song before the Lord, he comes, and he establishes his throne upon the praise of his people." So, here we are. We're already gathered together in his name, and there's this increased manifestation, but something happens as we turn our hearts towards him, and we declare his goodness. We sing his praises. He comes yet again in another wave, another level, another measure of presence.

You know, David made this statement. He says, "When I come into your house ..." He says, "I look for your power and your glory." Those are two manifestations of presence: power, glory. Two sides of the same coin, "power and glory." I'd exhort you, when you come together with the saints this place, in your homes, over lunch, doesn't matter where it is, look for how he will manifest himself at that moment because he promised us. He made a covenant with his disciples, and that covenant was passed on to every believer, everyone who puts their faith in Christ. In John 14, he said, "I will manifest myself to you." It means, "I will make myself conspicuous." You won't miss me if you're looking for me.

So, here's this generosity of God in just revealing presence to you and me. So, we lift praises to him, and yet there's just more and more waves of presence and glory that just invades the room, invades the air. There's such a power present right now that just anything at all could happen, anything at all.

Yet we have this additional bit of insight that comes from scripture. It's an unusual verse. It's an unusual word in Isaiah, chapter 6, where Isaiah the prophet is standing there, and he makes this statement. He says, "I see the Lord. He's high and lifted up, and the train of his robe filled the temple. It gives the picture that he just came into the building, but he's still coming. He's here, but there's more of Him coming. He's going to get more of Him into the room.

I don't know what you do with that, but that starts messing me up. Like, he's here, but there's more coming? It's like if you could just imagine the long robe as somebody comes into the room that they continue to pull that robe of his presence into the room. That's exactly what's happening as we hunger for him. There's just a drawing of presence into the place. This is the father —— This is the perfect, perfect father.

See, the world became a planet of orphans, a planet of orphans, and Jesus came to do two basic things. One is to bear the penalty of sin so that we could experience number two, and that is to discover the perfect father. He came to manifest the perfect father, the ultimate father.

In what is called the Lord's Prayer, it's actually the Disciple's Prayer, but in Matthew 6, he says, "Our Father ..." Everything that Jesus did was to bring us to the place to be able to say our Father. Everything. Everything was focused on this one thing. "Our Father who art in heaven, hallowed be thy name, thy kingdom come." Here's the good news. It's the Father's kingdom. Everything about the kingdom that you long for comes from the Father, comes by, comes through connection with the Father who doesn't reject, the Father who heals every bit of brokenness.

Do you know why there's healing? Do you know why people's bodies get healed? Because that's the Father, the Father caring for his children. Do you know why deliverance comes? Yes, it doesn't exist in Heaven; we know that. We've prayed it, declared it, pursued that for years. He breaks off the torment of people's hearts and minds. It's true. He does it today, and he'll do it again today. But he does it because he's a Father, and he doesn't want his kids to be unclear in their thinking, in their appreciation for life, the value for the moment that God has brought upon us, the love that he's offered to us, the experience that we have.

It's not a Sunday experience; it's a right now experience. It's the fact that right now, at this moment, I get to taste and see that the Lord is good. I get to taste and see that he's a perfect Father, absolutely perfect as a Father. "Our Father who art in heaven, hallowed be thy name, thy kingdom," that everything that we long for in life is connected to the kingdom of the perfect Father. Everything that we've ever ached for in life, everything that we've ever valued that was there because of things that he put in us. Everything is connected to a relationship with the perfect Father, the Father who has never rejected anyone, the Father who is the divine yes. All of his promises are yes and amen.

Even Jesus came to reveal the Father. He did so powerfully that Isaiah called him the everlasting Father. He said in John, chapter 17 ... He says, "I have manifested your name." He carried the name, the weightiness of the Father's glory into the earth so that humanity could no longer be orphaned, that there would be a true, heart-to-heart spirit connection between every person and the Father. Absolute acceptance. He's better than you think, so we have to change the way we think.

You know, the Lord is working to build up a company of people that walk-in maturity. He does want us to be strong and stable as spiritual mothers and fathers, but it takes a good son to be a good fa-ther ... and it's never too late to learn what it is to be a son, to be a child. Everyone comes into this king-dom as a child, everyone. No grownups welcome here. Everyone comes in as a child. That's the way it works. That's what it means to be born again. So, he's working out his perfect, master plan by knitting you together with other people that are on the same journey, discovering what it is to have a perfect Father.

I realize some people that are reading this were raised under such horrible abuse and neglect, but I've got really good news for you. Nobody has had a perfect father. Get over it. He being God is perfect. He makes up for all those people weren't. I mean, I had a father that was good, but our heavenly father is so much more than any earthly father could be, so just get over it. Give up your right to use your past as an excuse for what you don't taste of today. Give up, just bury it. It's not as though... an empty philosophy that just is supposed to pump you up to make you feel good for a day or something. It's an ongoing, living encounter with the perfect Father that is fully trustworthy. There's nothing about it ... There's not even a shadow in heaven. He is so filled with light and so everywhere that there are no shadows. There's no shade of darkness anywhere in him, and he wants that revealed. He wants that known. He wants that seen.

My hope, my cry, is that we as the people of God, would honestly learn to walk in the fullness of who he is. Is it possible? I hope so. I have nothing else to do with my life, so that's the only direction I have to go in is to learn to carry that presence and that Father heart towards people, that Father heart towards this planet that was orphaned so long ago.

I was looking at Ephesians 3, where it says, "For this reason, I bow my knees before the father of our Lord Jesus Christ, from whom the whole family in Heaven and on Earth derives its name." We derive our identity, our sense of purpose, our sense of history ... History and purpose give you momentum for success. Your history ...

Your last name... I mean, now in the natural, my last name is Vincent. There's been a whole bunch of them before me. So, there is this momentum. They gave me a first name; they gave me potential. The potential is according to how I yield my heart, how I navigate life. Now, the Lord God chose you by name, and he gave you his name, so you have an eternal history, which is a pretty good track record. And he's given you your name. We won't get into it now, but I do believe everybody in the things of

God has a name that God calls you that you may not be aware of.

But you inherit his name. You are born again. You have your name, and he gives you a purpose and a destiny from whom every family in Heaven and on Earth derives its name. In Heaven and on Earth. Same purpose. When God looks at the Church, all got their name, their sense of purpose and identity, from the Father. Jealous Christians just don't know who they are. You would never be jealous of somebody else if you knew who you were. You would never want somebody else's gift if you knew why you were alive. And it all comes from the Father.

Romans 8 has the greatest prayer meeting in the universe. There's never been a greater prayer meeting than in this chapter. Verse 14 says, "As many as are led by the spirit of God, these are the sons of God." Verse 15: "You did not receive the spirit of bondage again to fear, but you received the spirit of adoption by whom we cry out, 'Abba, Father.'" Say it with me. Abba, father. Say it again. Abba, father. The whole focus and point of this chapter are that right there. It's that humanity, you as an individual, get restored to God and can say, "Abba, father."

The Spirit himself bears witness with our spirit that we are children of God. And if we are children, then we are heirs, heirs of God, joint-heirs with Christ. If we indeed suffer with him that we may be glorified together. Verse 18: "I consider that the sufferings of this present time are not worthy to be compared with the glory which shall be revealed in us. For the earnest expectation of creation eagerly waits for the revealing of the Sons of God." So, the entire focus here of the spirit of God... Now, creation itself is mirroring the cry of Heaven for the sons, the daughters of God, to be revealed for who they are because they finally learned who they are.

Jump over to verse 22. "For we know that the whole creation groans and labors with birth pangs until now." For what? For you to be revealed as a child of God, someone who knows the father. Verse 23: "Not only that, but we also who have the firstfruits of the spirit, even we ourselves groan within ourselves, eagerly waiting for the adoption, the redemption of our body." What do we have here? We have all of the creation groaning and travailing. It's a prayer expression. Deep intercession is going on by all creation for you to learn who you are so you can be revealed who you are, that he can be revealed through you.

It's a good prayer meeting. We've got creation praying, and we've got, in verse 23, all the saints groaning and travailing with the same focus. We get down to verse 26. "Likewise, the Spirit helps us in our weaknesses. We do not know what we should pray for as we ought, but the Spirit himself makes intercession for us with groanings which cannot be uttered." So, we've got all of creation praying. We've got the saints groaning and travailing in prayer. Now, we've got the Holy Spirit joining in the prayer meeting. This is a good prayer meeting.

Creation groans and travails in the chorus for the revelation of the sons and daughters of God. The sons and daughters of God groan and travail for the completion of what they've experienced. The Holy Spirit groans and travails for the same thing. And then we jump over to verse 34. "Who is he who condemns? It is Christ who died, furthermore is also risen, who is even at the right hand of God who also makes intercession for us." Now, is this not the greatest prayer meeting in the universe? We've got every created thing groaning and travailing. Why? Just for you.

We've got our own hearts to cry out. There are times where there's this sense of presence that comes upon you. It'll be in worship, and you have known words. You don't even know what to do. You're just so aware of God, and your spirit, man, just begins to groan and to travail. For what? For that. They're all focused on one thing. The Father must be manifest in His Sons, in His daughters. The father must be seen for who he is. And so, creation groans. The saints groan. The Holy Spirit groans. The Son of God at the right hand of the Father groans and travails all for the same thing. The Earth has been orphaned. Humanity has been orphaned. And there is the fight for identity, fight for possession, fight for progress, fight all over the planet to get what he offers for free.

When the Bible says, "Don't give a thought about tomorrow. Tomorrow will take care of itself. Don't be wrapped up in grabbing for yourself," he's trying to sever us from that orphan spirit that needs to somehow build an identity by gathering to ourselves security that money can't provide, that extra food on the plate just can't provide. It doesn't bring what's needed. There's the cry in the heart for identity. There's the cry in the heart to belong. There's the cry in the heart for purpose.

The heart of humanity aches for these things, and it's all wrapped up in the connection to the perfect, heavenly Father. He heals because he's Father. He delivers because he's a perfect Father. He embraces. He accepts. Before anybody deserves it, that's what he does: he accepts. He accepts people long before they could ever earn it, long before we could ever do anything to do right to please him. He's just not that kind of a father.

Sometimes we come to the Lord. We know we got there by grace, and then somehow many people have thought, after we got saved, God became angry. We were won by his love, but somehow, we were to be kept by his anger. That's a lie. The grace that brought you is the grace that will keep you. It's all about this father. All the insecurities, all the fears, everything that he deals with, he would take no thought about tomorrow, when he would teach Jesus to work with his disciplines.

You know, you have to remember Jesus came to reveal the Father. Everything that he did, he did as the Father. Everything he did. The woman caught in adultery... The way he treated her was as the heavenly Father. Jesus made it clear. He says, "If you've seen me, you've seen the Father." "If you've seen me, you've seen the Father. The Father and I are one." He was the one, says he's the perfect, perfect representation of the Father's nature, an exact representation of the Father's nature. He, in fact, is the presence that emanates from the Father. It's the truth.

So, then we go about life. Everything we do for people is just to try to get them to discover the Father. Striving for a Christian only exists in the absence of realizing the Father's love. All the striving, the competition, the fear, the anxiety, all of it can only exist where there's an absence of the tasting of the Father's love.

Kind of the hard part of all this for us is that it's so ridiculously good, and it's so ridiculously perfect, that we want to figure out some way to earn it, or somehow make ourselves better suited for it. That's a strange paradox in the scripture. It says, "He who sends much loves much." What it doesn't say is you have to send much to love much. He just says, for some reason, those who are in the biggest mess and they know they couldn't get themselves, they have the liberty to love God more than others. So, the answer isn't going deeper into sin to taste of his love. The answer is to realize how deep in sin you were and that the most dreadful sin of all is the sin of religion because it keeps people anesthetized under the influence of anesthesia, deadened to the real need.

I really believe it's the reason the Lord has empha-sized for us in the responsibilities increase, and be-cause responsibility increases, there's a greater and... Greater and greater need for biblical government and all these things. So, we search the scriptures, and we just keep coming back to this one thing. The moment we leave the concept of family, we have left the concept of the kingdom. Why? Because it's the father's kingdom.

It's a kingdom built around a perfect father. That's why we pray. "Give us this day our daily bread." Because the perfect father provides for his kids, it's a kingdom where provision is to be ac-cepted.

But the point is that the father is looking for those who know their sons, where you can look at the one who stole from you for so long. You can look at every lie that you've ever believed, and you can say, "Watch this."

Put your hand on your heart. Let's just pray. Father, I do pray that you would continue to restore us as a people to the father's heart, to the perfect father. We thank you for what you're saying. We thank you for what you're doing. Lord, what I ask is that you help us to hear the groaning of creation, the travail of the spirit, the intercessions of the son of God, that we might join in chorus with the true revelation of what you're doing on this planet, restoring a planet of orphans to a perfect father. We just say, "Yes, Lord." We do. We just say yes. We say yes to all you have purposed and planned for us. We say, "Yes, Lord." "Yes, Lord." "Yes, Lord." Amen.

About the Author

Bill Vincent is no stranger to understanding the power of God. Not only has he spent over twenty years as a Minister with a strong prophetic anointing, but he is now also an Apostle and Author with Revival Waves of Glory Ministries in Litchfield, IL. Along with his wife, Tabitha, he leads a team providing apostolic oversight in all aspects of ministry, including service, personal ministry, and Godly character.

Bill offers a wide range of writings and teachings from deliverance, to experiencing the presence of God and developing Apostolic cutting-edge Church structure. Drawing on the power of the Holy Spirit through years of experience in Revival, Spiritual Sensitivity, and deliverance ministry, Bill now focuses mainly on pursuing the Presence of

God and breaking the power of the devil off of people's lives.

His books 50 and counting has since helped many people to overcome the Spirits and curses of Satan. For more information or to keep up with Bill's latest releases, please visit revivalwavesofgloryministries.com. To contact Bill, feel free to follow him on twitter @revivalwaves.

Recommended Books

By Bill Vincent
Overcoming Obstacles
Glory: Pursuing God's Presence
Defeating the Demonic Realm
Increasing Your Prophetic Gift
Increase Your Anointing
Keys to Receiving Your Miracle
The Supernatural Realm
Waves of Revival
Increase of Revelation and Restoration
The Resurrection Power of God
Discerning Your Call of God
Apostolic Breakthrough
Glory: Increasing God's Presence
Love is Waiting – Don't Let Love Pass You By
The Healing Power of God
Glory: Expanding God's Presence

Receiving Personal Prophecy
Signs and Wonders
Signs and Wonders Revelations
Children Stories
The Rapture
The Secret Place of God's Power
Building a Prototype Church
Breakthrough of Spiritual Strongholds
Glory: Revival Presence of God
Overcoming the Power of Lust
Glory: Kingdom Presence of God
Transitioning to the Prototype Church
The Stronghold of Jezebel
Healing After Divorce
A Closer Relationship With God
Cover Up and Save Yourself
Desperate for God's Presence
The War for Spiritual Battles
Spiritual Leadership
Global Warning
Millions of Churches
Destroying the Jezebel Spirit
Awakening of Miracles
Deception and Consequences Revealed
Are You a Follower of Christ

Don't Let the Enemy Steal from You!
A Godly Shaking
The Unsearchable Riches of Christ
Heaven's Court System
Satan's Open Doors
Armed for Battle
The Wrestler
Spiritual Warfare: Complete Collection
Growing In the Prophetic
Faith
The Angry Fighter's Story
Understanding Heaven's Court System

Web Site:
www.revivalwavesofgloryministries.com

RWG Publishing

President/Bill Vincent
https://rwgpublishing.com/

Bookstore: https://aerbook.com/store/
RWG_Publishing
Twitter:

https://twitter.com/PublishingRwg

Youtube: https://www.youtube.com/channel/
UCROlJ7vUB3m2e6T39c0G9ag?view_as=sub-
scriber